Paw Prints on my Heart

journal belongs to...

© 2016 Ranch House Press
All rights reserved. Printed in the United States of America.

www.annettebridges.com

ISBN: 978-1-946371-04-1

Journal Prompts

Paw Prints on my Heart

1. What can animals teach us?
2. Do you have pets now? Write about each animal's strengths and weaknesses. Then write about your strengths and weaknesses as a pet owner.
3. Write a poem dedicated to your pet.
4. Who was your favorite childhood pet and why? Talk about some of your experiences with this pet and why you'll always keep him or her in your memory.
5. Imagine your pet was a cartoon character? Who would it be? What kind of adventures would he or she have?
6. What are your pet's favorite things – toys, treats, places to walk, blankets, sleeping spots?
7. Finish this sentence: "If I were an animal, I would be a _____, and I would…."'
8. If someone were to care for your pet while you were away, what things would they need to know?
9. What would your day be like if you were your pet?
10. What have you learned from living with your pet?
11. Imagine the world if it was ruled by your pet. Make a list that would be true. If (your pet's name) ruled the world…Examples: Stealing dirty socks would never be a crime or The trash can would be considered a goodie box or Belly rubs would be given every hour.
12. Print up your favorite pet photos and include captions that tell the story of your memories with your furry friend.
13. Do you talk with your pet? Jot down three conversations you typically have with him or her.
14. Make a list of the five most memorable things your pet did with you or another human during the past month.
15. Jot down five of the funniest things your pet has ever done.
16. Jot down five things your pet did that got him or her in big trouble.
17. What is your first memory with your pet? Describe the first time you met.
18. Describe identifiable features, quirks or personality traits of your pet that you noticed early on or that grew over time.
19. How does your pet make you feel?
20. Describe ways in which your pet has inspired, enlightened or informed you.
21. List things you want to always remember about your pet.
22. Make a list of the words your pet knows and understands.
23. Make a list of favorite activities you and your pet enjoy together.
24. If your pet could write you a letter, what would he or she say to you right now?
25. What are the top ten tips to keep your pet happy on a road-trip?
26. If your pet could write a letter to Santa Claus, what would he or she wish for Christmas?
27. What is the single most endearing thing about your pet?
28. What is the single most frustrating thing about your pet?
29. What do you think your pet does when you're not home?
30. Write a biography for your pet. Write in first person as if your pet was speaking.
31. Your pet needs to write a letter of recommendation for you. What would he or she say?

color your world

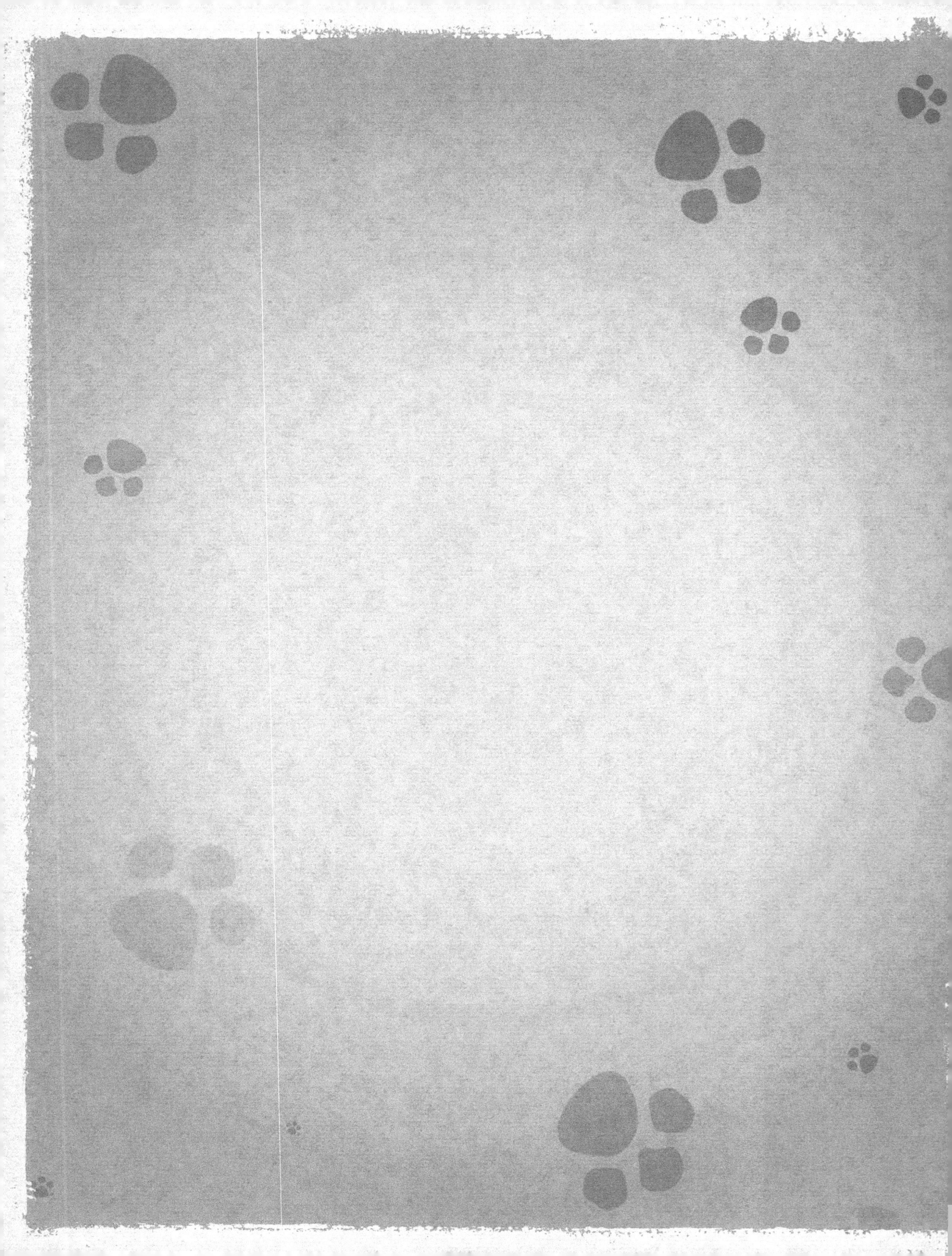

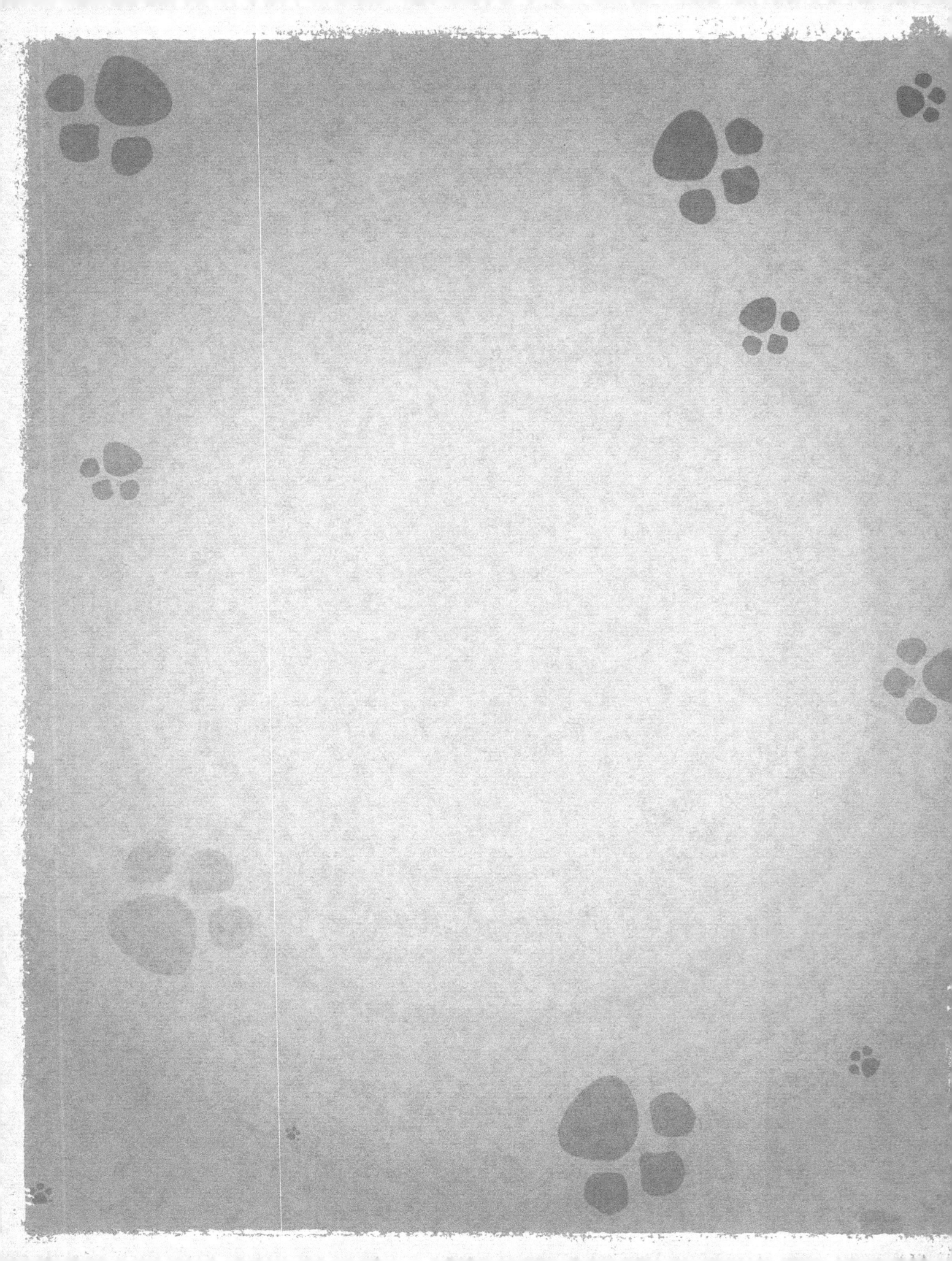

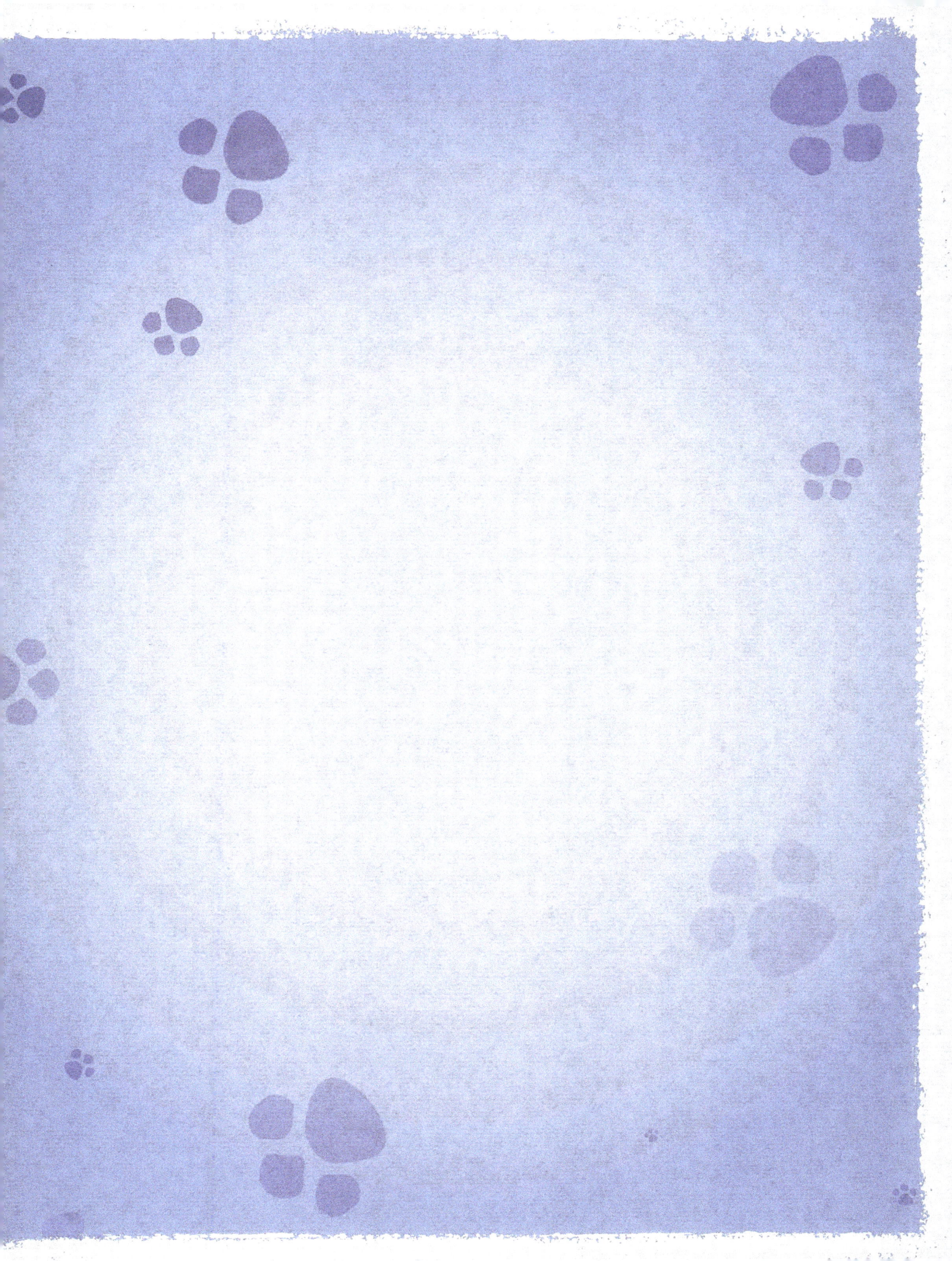

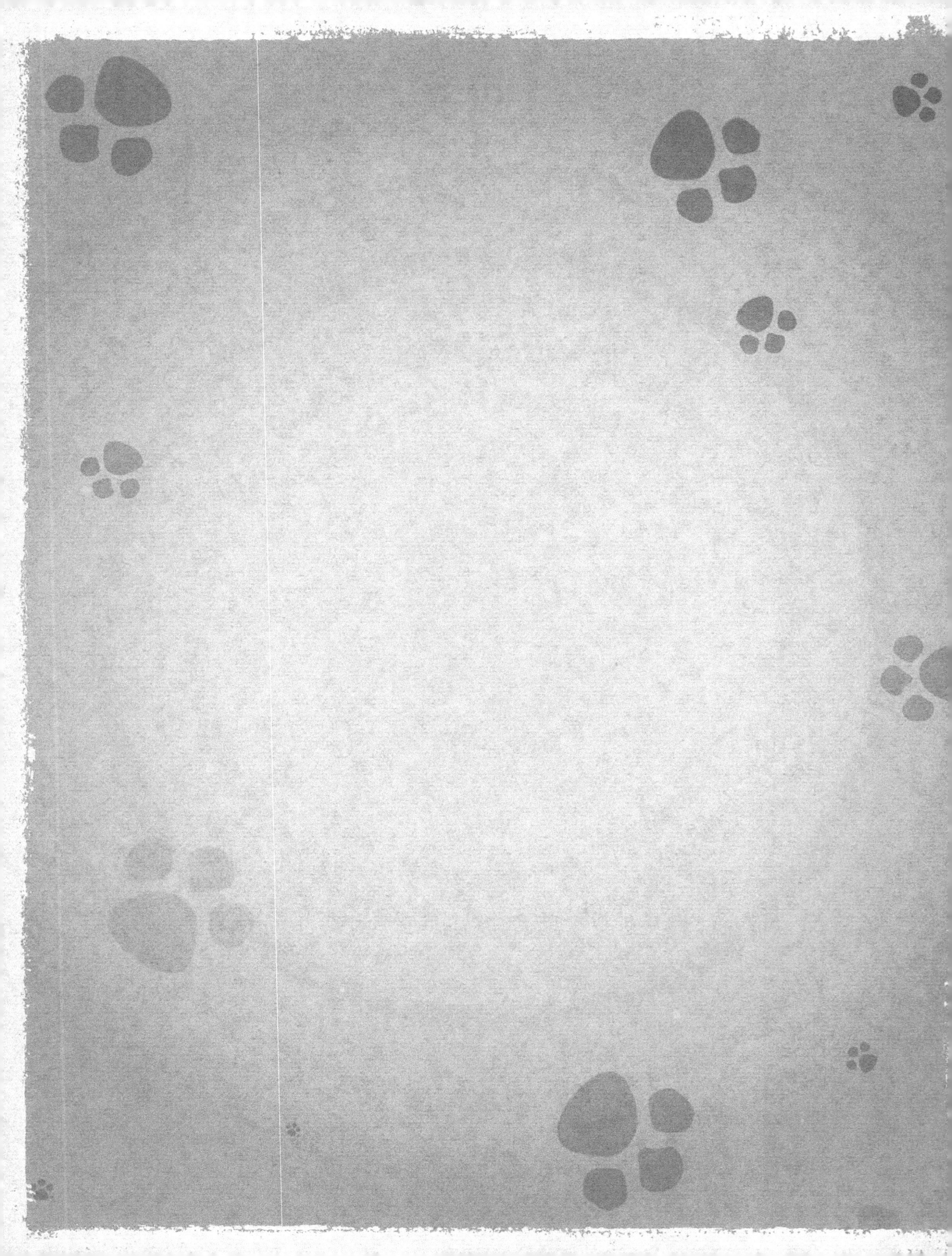

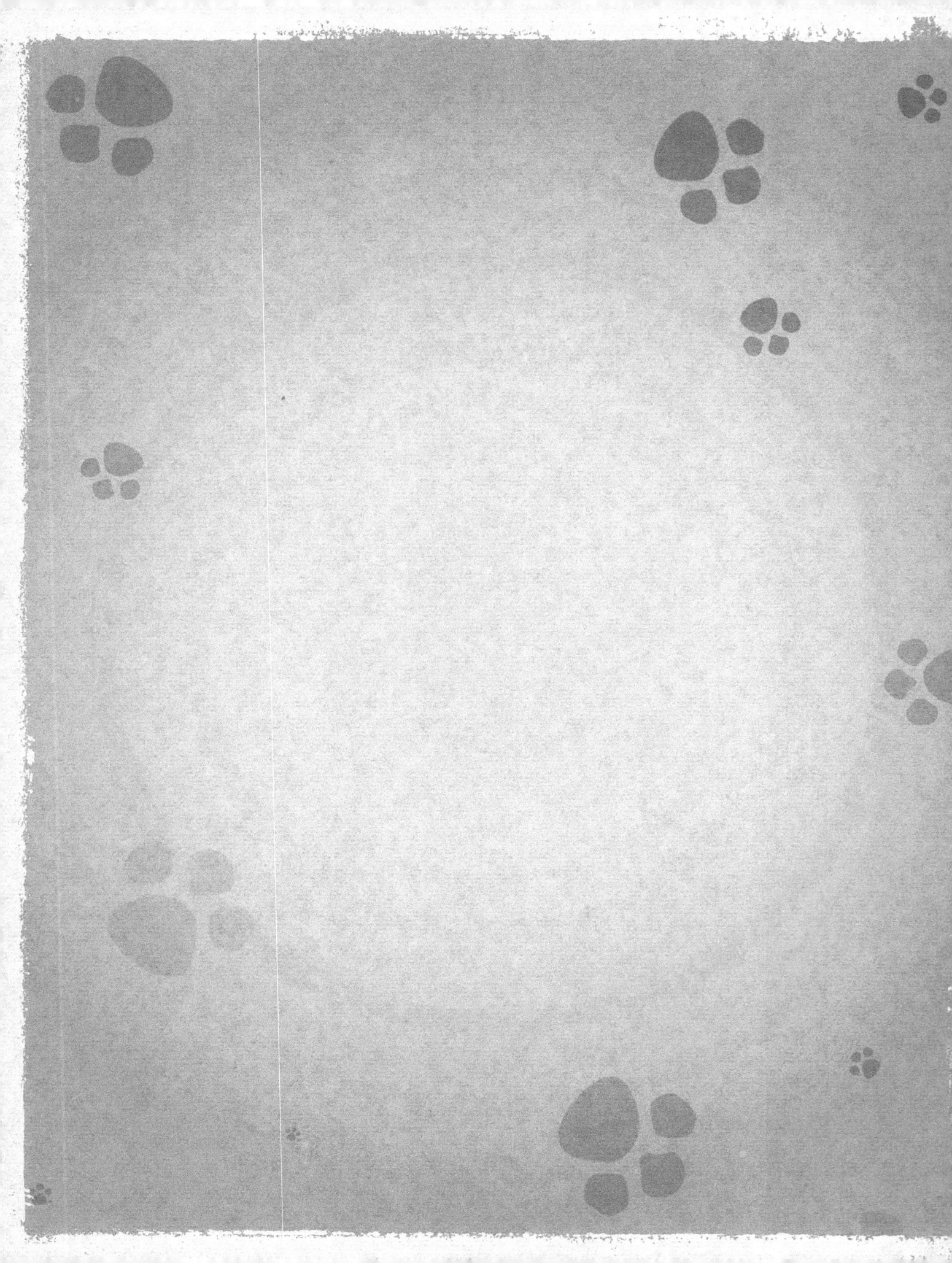

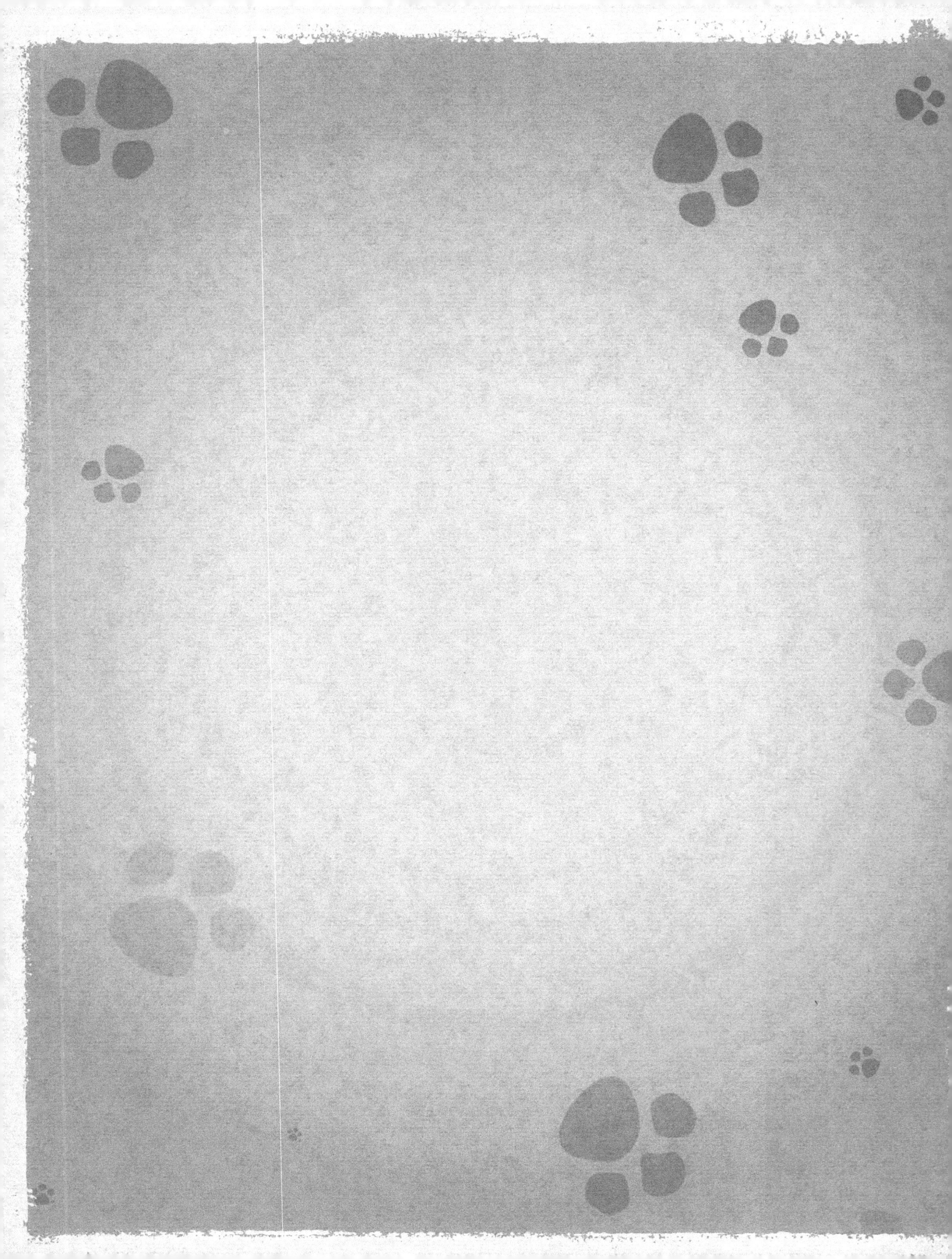

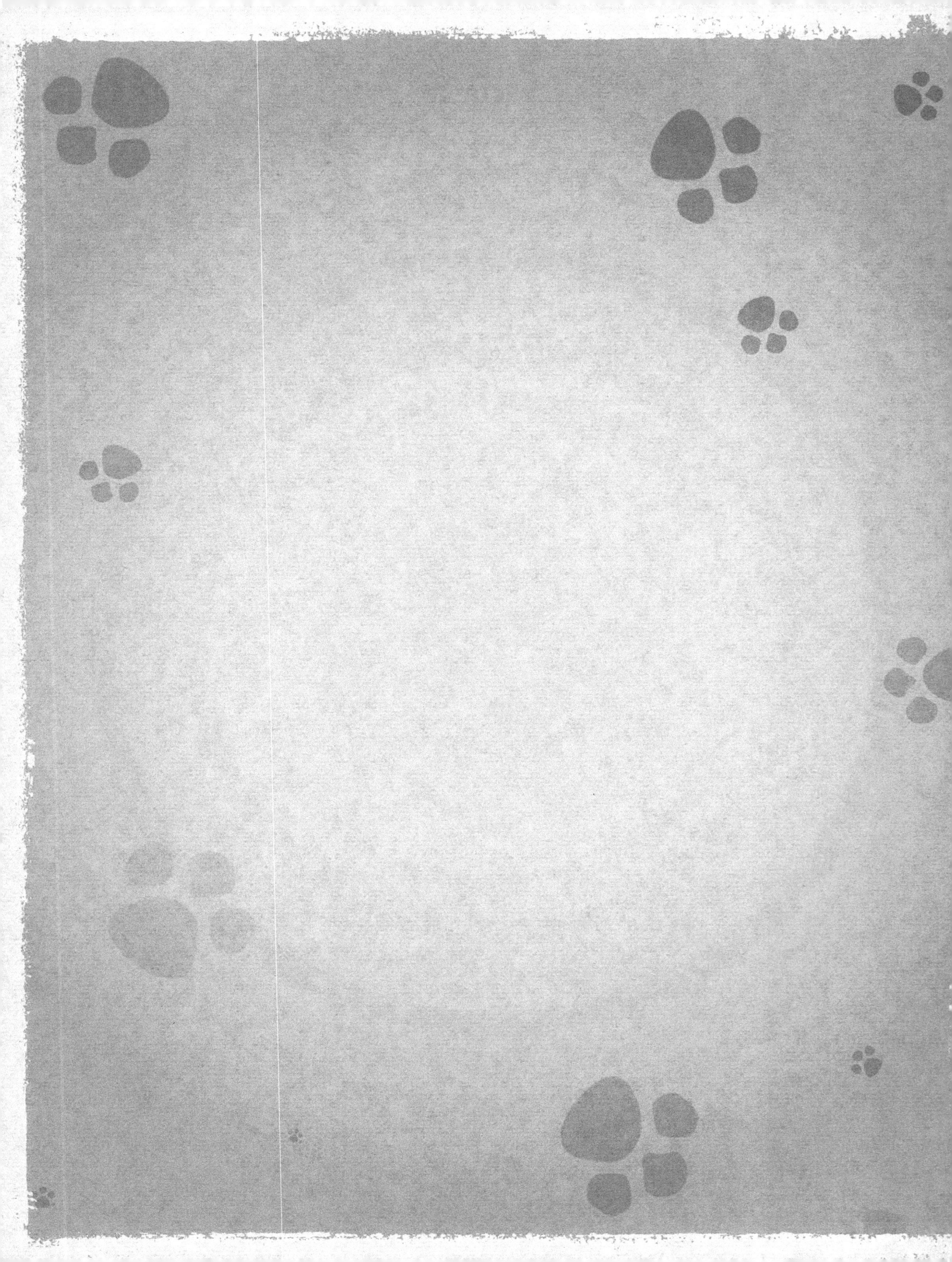

ABOUT the CREATOR

Annette Bridges is an author, publisher and women's retreat host on a mission to help every woman realize her story is extraordinary, valuable and noteworthy.

She has published the ***Color Your World Journal Series*** and formed a journal club to provide community, support and tools for women to record their ideas, feelings, experiences, memories and all the important details of their lives.

Before writing books and publishing journals and coloring books, this former public school and homeschool educator spent a decade writing hundreds of helpful, instructive, and light-hearted columns published by Texas newspapers, parenting magazines, websites and bloggers.

Annette lives on a Texas cattle ranch with her husband John, dachshund Lady and lots of cows. She can drive a tractor but only if wearing a fresh coat of lipstick and it's not her pedicure day!

You can learn more about Annette's books and products, blogs and videos as well as her women's retreats and other events at www.annettebridges.com.

Look for her on social media, too!

MESSAGE from the PUBLISHER

The **Color Your World Journal Series** is a pathway to self-discovery. It's where you write notes to yourself. Be your own cheerleader. Give yourself encouragement. Tell yourself what you're grateful for. Celebrate you!

There are countless reasons to keep a journal including collecting favorite recipes, listing goals and celebrating every experience and every one that's near and dear to you. A journal provides a home for the memories and lessons learned that you never want to forget.

Why a niche journal?

If you're anything like me, you have a journal (or even two or three journals) where you write anything and everything about anything and everything. My challenge comes when trying to find something I've written. I flip and flip through the pages of my two, three or four journals trying to find whatever it is. I never remember which journal I wrote down my whatever's!!

The solution? A niche journal! A journal that has a specific focus and theme! A journal where you can record your ideas, inspirations and things you want to remember in the appropriate journal.

Why big unlined paper?

Because big unlined paper is needed to record big ideas, dreams and memories! You need room to grow, stretch and expand. You need space to think beyond the confines of what you've always done, to pursue new dreams, discover your power and reimagine your purpose again and again. You need pages without lines and limitations to reconnect with your creative, perfectly imperfect self.

Plus, big unlined paper gives you space for more than words. You have plenty of room to doodle, draw or post photographs and clippings, too.

Why color is important?

When you journal, use colored pens and markers! Your world doesn't happen in black and white. Your life should be lived and written about in many colors. Even dark and sad memories feel lighter and brighter when told in color.

Journaling in color affects your mood and perception of your world. Colors evoke calm, cheer and comfort. Using color can lift your spirit and inspire your imagination. You may be surprised by all the beautiful benefits from adding more color into your life story.

When journaling, give yourself time to listen to your heart and reflect. Breathe in the moments. Feel. Be quiet. Let yourself be totally and thoroughly present with your thoughts. Let your heart transform you and teach you new insights. Open your mind to consider new ideas and possibilities. You may find that what your heart teaches will be life changing.

www.ingramcontent.com/pod-product-compliance
Lightning Source LLC
Chambersburg PA
CBHW051253110526
44588CB00025B/2977